Steve

PRESENTED TO

Helen

FROM

Easter 2022

DATE

The GIFT of the CROSS

Embracing the Promise of the Resurrection

CHARLES F. STANLEY

THOMAS NELSON
Since 1798

Published in Nashville, Tennessee, by Thomas Nelson. Thomas Nelson is a registered trademark of HarperCollins Christian Publishing, Inc.

Thomas Nelson titles may be purchased in bulk for educational, business, fund-raising, or sales promotional use. For information, please email SpecialMarkets@ThomasNelson.com.

Unless otherwise noted, all Scripture quotations are taken from the New American Standard Bible® (NASB). Copyright © 1960, 1962, 1963, 1968, 1971, 1972, 1973, 1975, 1977, 1995, 2020 by The Lockman Foundation. Used by permission. www.Lockman.org

Scripture quotations marked NKJV are taken from the New King James Version®. Copyright © 1982 by Thomas Nelson. Used by permission. All rights reserved.

Scripture quotations marked NLT are taken from the Holy Bible, New Living Translation. Copyright © 1996, 2004, 2015 by Tyndale House Foundation. Used by permission of Tyndale House Ministries, Carol Stream, Illinois 60188. All rights reserved.

Any internet addresses, phone numbers, or company or product information printed in this book are offered as a resource and are not intended in any way to be or to imply an endorsement by Thomas Nelson, nor does Thomas Nelson vouch for the existence, content, or services of these sites, phone numbers, companies, or products beyond the life of this book.

Cover design by Shane Kingery.
Interior design by Kristy Edwards.
Images used under license from Shutterstock.com.

ISBN 978-1-4002-3251-2 (audiobook)
ISBN 978-1-4002-3249-9 (eBook)
ISBN 978-1-4002-3245-1 (HC)

Printed in China

22 23 24 25 26 GRI 10 9 8 7 6 5 4 3 2 1

CONTENTS

THE POWER OF THE RESURRECTION FOR YOU

INTRODUCTION

What a Gift

*The word of the cross is foolishness to
those who are perishing, but to us who are
being saved it is the power of God.*

1 CORINTHIANS 1:18

*I*s the cross truly . . . a *gift?*

We may say it is and even have an understanding of what we have received. But when we think about Jesus on the cross—the beatings He received, the blood He spent, the wood tearing at His open wounds, the crown of thorns piercing His brow—we might wonder at what kind of gift it is. Like the personal trials we experience, which do not kill us but make us stronger, there *is* a blessing in it. But the blessing can be hard-won, and the pain we experience on earth can be intense as we carry our own crosses. We may approach the place where Christ sacrificed Himself to save us and question if it were indeed a gift at all.

In a sense, this is why "the word of the cross is foolishness to those who are perishing" (1 Corinthians 1:18). Can such pain *really* bring us a blessing?

We may wear crosses as jewelry and decorate our homes with them, but a Christian in the early church would never have hung one around his or her neck. To do so would be the equivalent of donning an electric-chair charm on a necklace today. The cross was a symbol of horror to the early believers and citizens of the Roman Empire. This was because crucifixion was one of the most painful forms of

We have lost the reality of how much was suffered for us on the cross and, therefore, how profoundly Jesus understands and has compassion for our pain.

execution and the ultimate symbol of torment, shame, and death, reserved for the worst criminals.

On the one hand, we have lost the reality of how much Jesus suffered for us on the cross and, therefore, how profoundly He understands and has compassion for our pain. On the other, we may not truly comprehend what He purchased for us. I believe that this may be one of the main reasons many Christians live in defeat—because they haven't truly grasped what Jesus accomplished on the cross for them. We may talk about it, we may sing about it, and we may even believe something supernatural occurred on the cross, but do we recognize how what Jesus did there has the power to transform our identity, nature, and relationship with the living God? Do we truly realize the message of the cross that the Father has given to us through Scripture? Or is the cross something we just talk about?

We may know the message of the cross preached every Sunday in churches around the world: Holy God, seeing humanity in our helpless condition because of the sin that separates us from Him, set a plan in motion that would take centuries to carry out and that would culminate in Him becoming human flesh through His Son, Jesus. After living a sinless life, Jesus died on a Roman cross as a substitutionary sacrifice for the sins of all people—paying the price that our sin demanded, opening the way for us to know the Lord, and giving us a home in heaven. Jesus was buried and rose again three days later, the resurrection demonstrating that God the Father accepted Christ's death as sufficient to save us. This is the heart of the Christian message—the hope of all humanity. The cross of Jesus is central to everything you and I believe as Christians.

Yet the apostle Paul had even more to say about the significance of the cross. In Galatians 6:14–15 he wrote, "Far be it from me to boast, except in the cross of our Lord Jesus Christ, through which the world has been crucified to me, and I to the world. For neither is circumcision anything, nor uncircumcision, but a new creation." What Paul was talking about here is how he used to live by a well-established set of rules—which most of us do. The Jewish people were identified by circumcision and would either be respected as godly or shamed as ungodly by how they followed the laws of Moses.

Perhaps you can relate to this. There are things you and I do, or paths we take, for which we immediately condemn ourselves and feel unworthy or shameful. Or perhaps there are particular successes, achievements, or activities in our lives that give us a feeling of

The cross of Jesus is central to everything you and I believe as Christians.

The cross is the one and only bridge that connects us to the One who rules heaven and earth.

superiority—but their value wavers when we see our accomplishments overshadowed or when those pious disciplines become a burden.

But what happens through the cross is that you and I become brand-new creatures—with a new identity, power, heritage, and way of seeing circumstances and dealing with situations. As Paul wrote, "If anyone is in Christ, this person is a new creation; the old things passed away; behold, new things have come" (2 Corinthians 5:17). The cross changes absolutely everything. We go from relying solely on our own resources to having the living God guide and help us. This is why "to us who are being saved [the cross] is the power of God" (1 Corinthians 1:18). It is the one and only bridge that connects us to the One who rules heaven and earth.

Now, I realize that there may be some Christians reading this who will say, "Yes, but all the rules I live by come from the Bible, and I still experience hardship and defeat, and I feel somewhat imprisoned by it all." I would ask you to take a long look at the rules you live by, list them out on a sheet of paper, and then note beside each one where it is found in God's Word and if it fits the context of the scriptural passage. You may find that not all of them are as biblical as you think, but they may instead be due to some church or denominational preferences or faulty theology. I would also encourage you to ask yourself the questions, "Am I following these rules to earn God's acceptance and approval or to prove myself to Him? Am I doing so to maintain a level of respectability or honor with my church or another group?" Because if you are, then you may not have a complete understanding of what Jesus did on the cross for you. By all means, please keep reading.

Friend, what Paul is saying is that the cross has a twofold message, and the problem with Christians is that often we have seen only one side of it. We have seen the aspect that deals with our sins—and we should be exceedingly grateful for it. But we have not examined the side that deals with our new life. Wherever Paul went, he talked about the fact that God "raised us up with Him, and seated us with Him in the heavenly places in Christ Jesus" (Ephesians 2:6). The cross was not a decoration to Paul; rather, it was the *beginning of life*—a higher life, a more powerful, meaningful, and significant life. Christ's sacrifice on the cross not only redeems us from the penalty of our sins and changes our future destination but transforms us and gives us real, tangible hope here and now.

I believe that this brand-new, resurrection power–filled life is

Christ's sacrifice on the cross not only redeems us from the penalty of our sins and changes our future destination, but it transforms us and gives us real, tangible hope here and now.

what many people are longing for but what many people miss. And the reason they miss it is because they want to know about the cross in a general sense, but they don't want to get too close to it. You see, the closer you get to the cross, the more you realize what you're doing that keeps you from experiencing the new life the Lord has for you.

It is the struggle Paul talks about in Romans 7: "I want to do what is right, but I can't. I want to do what is good, but I don't. I don't want to do what is wrong, but I do it anyway. . . . I have discovered this principle of life—that when I want to do what is right, I inevitably do what is wrong" (vv. 18–19, 21 NLT). Have you ever experienced this frustrating struggle? That is the sin nature still at work in you. Yet Paul also lets you know that "the answer is in Jesus Christ our Lord. . . . Now there is no condemnation for those who belong to Christ Jesus. And because you belong to him, the power of the life-giving Spirit has freed you from the power of sin that leads to death" (Romans 7:25–8:2 NLT).

Jesus has set you free, but you must come to the end of yourself, whereby you are willing to say, "Lord, You have permission to do anything with my life You want to do." This doesn't mean abiding by a new set of laws and rules. Instead, it signifies living in a relationship with the living God, where you acknowledge that He knows best how to usher you into the new life He has for you.

Would you like Him to do so? If so, I invite you to come take a closer look at the cross with me, because the cross is key to understanding God's plan. In the following pages, we will examine Jesus' journey to the cross, be encouraged by its life-giving and identity-transforming message, and take hold of the awesome resurrection power that comes from being alive in Christ. Let's find out together what an extraordinary gift the cross truly is.

Because the truth of the matter is that the Lord Jesus Christ—God incarnate—chose to endure the cross for you. He decided to bear that humiliating, horrifically painful death that was reserved for the worst offenders because that's how deeply He loves you. He did so because He understood the profound hopelessness you experience when you are separated from the Father. He did so because that excruciating death was less painful than being separated from you for eternity. Isn't that a love worth examining? Hasn't He proven that He genuinely cares about you and gives whatever is necessary to lead you on the best path possible?

So take a good look at the cross. And the next time you feel unworthy or unlovable, remember what your Savior endured to rescue you, keep you safe for all eternity, and give you life at its very best. Recall what Jesus did to provide you with the only gift that truly changes everything for the better. He laid down His life willingly for you. And even now He holds nothing back so you can take up the life He has freely given you.

THE JOURNEY
to the CROSS

The cross has its power because of the One who shed His precious blood upon it. It is the place where the holy wrath and the abounding love of God intersect, so that we can be reconciled to Him and live eternally in His holy presence.

1

FROM THE
BEGINNING

God demonstrates His own love toward us, in that
while we were still sinners, Christ died for us.
ROMANS 5:8

*A*s human beings, we tend to interpret what happens to us through our experience—at times even missing the deepest root causes of our trials completely. For example, have you ever faced a difficulty and asked yourself, "What did I do to deserve this?" We know when a hardship occurs because we have messed up or have been selfish. But there are times when painful circumstances come out of the blue, having nothing to do with our choices. Such situations can leave us feeling confused, vulnerable, and, ultimately, powerless.

It may seem overly simplistic to attribute our suffering to living in a fallen world—a world characterized by a sin committed at the beginning of humankind by people we don't even know—but there is truth to it. One decision after another has been made and has brought us to where we are. From the moment Adam and Eve disobeyed God and broke fellowship with Him, nothing on this earth has been the same (Genesis 3). In fact, Romans 8:22 tells us, "The whole creation groans and suffers." There is no aspect of life as we know it that is unaffected by that first, eternity-shaking sin.

This is why the cross is so important. Some may believe the journey to the cross began on Palm Sunday, when Jesus rode into Jerusalem on a colt (Mark 11). Others may think He began His important mission when He was miraculously born to the virgin girl named Mary, on what we would today celebrate as Christmas. But the truth is that the journey to the cross began the moment Adam and Eve sinned. Romans 5:12 explains, "When Adam sinned, sin entered the world. Adam's sin brought death, so death spread to everyone, for everyone sinned" (NLT). Did you catch that? Sin brought *death*. Not only eventual physical death but *spiritual death*.

We receive our sinful nature and spiritual death at birth; it is passed on to us in an unbroken manner from Adam. This spiritual death we inherit means separation from God forever. Thankfully, He did not want that for us. The Father understands the pain and frustration you and I feel at not being able to reach Him, interact with Him, and receive His love because of our fallen human state—even when we don't recognize that is the source of our suffering. So, from that awful, eternity-altering moment in the garden of Eden, the Lord God set a plan in motion to bring us back to life—to save us from our sin and restore our relationship with Him.

Of course, our Creator understood that He would have to explain the path to us carefully. He realized that we would strive to come up with our own creative solutions to numb our pain and overcome

The Father understands the pain and frustration you and I feel at not being able to reach Him, interact with Him, and receive His love because of our fallen human state—even when we don't recognize that is the source of our suffering.

our hunger for relationship with Him. You see it in the now-famous quote from martial artist Morihei Ueshiba, who once philosophized, "There are many paths leading to the top of Mount Fuji." Many people believe that there are multiple ways of finding God—that life is a self-guided journey, and people are free to choose their own road to happiness. But Jesus was clear: there is only one way to find what we really need. In Luke 13:24, He said, "Strive to enter through the narrow door; for many, I tell you, will seek to enter and will not be able." In other words, there are people who will spend their lives chasing pursuits that cannot satisfy or save them, and they won't realize they've been on the wrong path until it's too late. What a sad, devastating thought.

This is why God was specific. He knew that other religions would arise that would falsely declare that they were the way to Him and put us to work for our redemption. So to protect us from their false assertions, the Lord gave us a living illustration that we would not be able to climb up to Him on our own or work our way to Him.

As you may recall, God chose the Jewish people to be His special nation through whom He would carry out His awesome plan of deliverance. So that the Israelites would be set apart and so other nations would know they were His (Deuteronomy 7:6), God gave them the Mosaic law. Through that law, the Lord established the sacrificial system as a provisional way for the people to enter into a relationship with Him. Remember: the original sin of Adam and Eve makes us dead spiritually and separates us from God. The Lord is holy, and sin cannot be in His presence. We also have our own transgressions, which likewise form a barrier to knowing Him. So the Lord instructed that each person must bring guilt offerings to the priest, who "shall make atonement for him before the Lord, and he will be forgiven for any one of the things which he may have done to incur guilt" (Leviticus 6:7). *Atonement* means "to cover." The idea was that these acceptable, predetermined sacrifices were the only manner to provisionally cover over sins from God.

While this sacrificial system functioned for a time, it was always temporary and inadequate in nature. Under the Levitical system, sins were forgiven, but the people still carried the burden of their sinful nature. In other words, they could not break free from evil impulses within them or from the way that internal evil destroyed them day by day. The wrongs they did were covered over—hidden—but they still felt guilty and dirty. And every time they violated the law, they would again be required to make an offering. Also, not all of their transgressions could be atoned for—such as certain deliberate violations of the law (Leviticus 4). Therefore, sin continued to have power over them no matter how good they tried to be.

Why? Because the blood of animals can never pay the whole debt incurred by our sin. Hebrews 10:3–4 confirms, "In those sacrifices there is a reminder of sins every year. For it is impossible for the blood of bulls and goats to take away sins." This is because sin holds on deep within us, creates a deficit we cannot fill, silently spreads, and devastates us. Because the sin nature is with us from birth, it goes far deeper than the surface issues we try to control, and it continually reminds us that we are imperfect, inadequate, broken, and marred. Sin hammers away at how we feel about ourselves until there is no money, sex, food, possession, entertainment, work, or anything in the world that can numb our pain.

Maybe you've experienced this yourself. Perhaps you've done everything you can to be good enough to reach God and be found acceptable to Him and to others. But you silently carry the awful burden of knowing what's really in your heart. It could be that like the Israelites, you have discovered that, ultimately, covering over sin doesn't work—it must be removed permanently.

Why did God provide a system that is inadequate to deal with our sinful nature? The answer is simple yet life-changing. He was providing "a shadow of the good things to come" (Hebrews 10:1). You see, the Lord had to show us once and for all that we could not be saved by our own efforts. He demonstrated that for us to have victory over sin, He had to do it for us. Only our holy, sinless Creator can truly take away our sin at the most profound parts of our being.

God is interested in more than retribution from us. He desires something more than getting paid back for the disobedience and disrespect we show Him when we sin. That's what many people think: that God is just a legalistic taskmaster who is looking for reasons to punish us.

But that is not the case at all. Instead, *the Father wants fellowship with us.* He is working to restore the relationship that was broken when humanity first walked away from Him. And He willingly paid the terrible penalty to rescue us from our sin and reconcile us to Him as only He could. Not forgiveness of sins one by one—but freedom from them once and for all (Hebrews 10:10).

The Father wants fellowship with us. He is working to restore the relationship that was broken when humanity first walked away from Him.

Who will set me free from the body of this death? Thanks be to God through Jesus Christ our Lord!

Romans 7:24–25

Likewise, through the sacrificial system, God was demonstrating that for sin to be removed forever, the ultimate price had to be paid—death would be required (Hebrews 9:22). But it could not be an ordinary death. Only by the death of One who was completely sinless could we be set free. That's why by His death on the cross and resurrection Jesus completely replaced our sinful nature with His righteousness—so we can have eternal fellowship with Him (2 Corinthians 5:17–19). He answers the question posed by the apostle Paul, "Who will set me free from the body of this death? Thanks be to God through Jesus Christ our Lord!" (Romans 7:24–25).

From the beginning and throughout history, God revealed His plan to heal the brokenness that plagues us by outlining the journey Jesus would take to the cross. Though there may be a multitude of roads to the earthly Mount Fuji, there's only one way to God—and that's by accepting Jesus Christ as your Lord and Savior (John 14:6; Acts 4:12). Christ offers the only path that leads to salvation. Though the world may offer an abundance of choices, they'll never lead to what you're really looking for (Proverbs 14:12). The only right choice is the one God offers—and that is through Jesus Christ. Though that path is the narrow one, it's always wide open to you.

2

ONLY JESUS

An angel of the Lord appeared to him in a dream, saying, "Joseph, son of David, do not be afraid to take Mary as your wife; for the Child who has been conceived in her is of the Holy Spirit. She will give birth to a Son; and you shall name Him Jesus, for He will save His people from their sins." Now all this took place so that what was spoken by the Lord through the prophet would be fulfilled: "Behold, the virgin will conceive and give birth to a Son, and they shall name Him Immanuel," which translated means, "God with us."

MATTHEW 1:20—23

*T*hroughout Scripture, we read the history of how the Lord set His awesome plan into motion. And Galatians 4:4–5 tells us, "When the fullness of the time came, God sent His Son, born of a woman, born under the Law, so that He might redeem those who were under the Law, that we might receive the adoption as sons and daughters." Apart from the crucifixion and resurrection, the birth of Jesus is the most important event in history—wrapped in the humility of the lowliest setting. It was the moment God came to earth to provide for our salvation. In that instance, a multitude of prophecies were fulfilled, countless prayers were answered, and our deepest hopes were realized.

But how can we know for sure that Jesus was the One? After all, many Jewish boys were born that year, and many people throughout history claimed to be great deliverers of humanity. Most of us know the heartbreak of trusting in the wrong person. It is devastating enough when we do so in love, business, medicine, finances, or some other aspect of our lives. But to make a mistake about who we trust with our souls for eternity? That is one person of whom we need to be absolutely certain.

From the beginning, the Lord put numerous signposts along the way so we could identify who the *Messiah*—or Anointed Savior—would be. Our Redeemer was foretold at the foundation of the world (Ephesians 1:3–5), affirmed at the fall of humanity (Genesis 3:15), reported by the prophets, and etched onto the very heart of Israel. For example, God announced that the Messiah would be a fulfillment of the covenant to Abraham and would come from his line (Genesis 12:3). And not only from Abraham—but a specific great-grandchild of Abraham, named Judah. Genesis 49:10 reports, "The scepter will not depart from Judah, nor the ruler's staff from between his feet, until Shiloh comes, and to him shall be the obedience of the peoples." The scepter was a symbol of authority, so the Lord was communicating that someone from the line of Judah would always be king of Israel. Also, the word *Shiloh* means "that which belongs to him." So Jewish scholars have taken this use of the word to refer to the Messiah; that, ultimately, the Deliverer would come through Judah's line.

Eventually, a monarch was born through Judah's line—a man named David, one of Israel's most famous kings. But God restricted the possibilities of who Christ would be even further when He told David, "Your house and your kingdom shall endure before Me forever; your throne shall be established forever" (2 Samuel 7:16)—indicating that the Redeemer would be his descendant. So the Messiah came to be known as the "Son of David" (Matthew 1:1 NKJV).

One after another, the Lord God provided astounding details about who our Savior would be (Isaiah 7:14; 11:1), where the Messiah would be born (Micah 5:2), when He would appear (Daniel 9:25–26), what He would do (Isaiah 61), and even His main region of ministry (Isaiah 9:1; Matthew 4:12–17). Thousands of these prophecies revealed the only One who could make us right with God—and that is Jesus.

Friend, our Savior could *only* be Jesus—only He fulfilled all that had been written about the One who would save us. And there would only be one sacrifice that He could make to fulfill the Lord's requirements, which was His death on the cross (Isaiah 53). Even that was fulfilled in precise detail.

Jesus is the One—the *only* One. Only Christ could carry the cross and make it into the bridge that would bring us back to God. In the fullness of time, Jesus came so that He might redeem us and make us His own. You don't have to wonder; God left all the signposts along the way so that you could know Him for sure.

$\mathcal{T}$housands of these prophecies revealed the only One who could make us right with God—and that is Jesus.

3

SOMETHING BETTER

This took place so that what was spoken through the prophet would be fulfilled:

"SAY TO THE DAUGHTER OF ZION,
'BEHOLD YOUR KING IS COMING TO YOU,
HUMBLE, AND MOUNTED ON A DONKEY,
EVEN ON A COLT, THE FOAL OF A DONKEY.'" . . .

*Most of the crowd spread their cloaks on the road, and others were cutting
branches from the trees and spreading them on the road. Now the crowds
going ahead of [Jesus], and those who followed, were shouting,*
"Hosanna to the Son of David;
BLESSED IS THE ONE WHO COMES IN THE NAME OF THE LORD;
Hosanna in the highest!"
MATTHEW 21:4–5, 8–9

Have you ever noticed that God doesn't always act as we expect Him to? In our limited, human thinking, we may imagine that all the indications are pointing to a certain way He will provide for us. And we can become very discouraged when something appears to go wrong, and He acts in a manner that is different from what we expect.

Never was this more apparent than on the day we call Palm Sunday. When Jesus entered Jerusalem during the last week of His life, the crowds received Him as the Deliverer-King they'd been waiting for—with palm branches and praises. Throughout their history, the Jews had interpreted the messianic promises as establishing an earthly empire for them rather than opening the kingdom of heaven. They believed that the Savior would come as a great warrior like King David and win back the lands that rightly belonged to Israel.

So when Jesus came into Jerusalem riding a colt, in fulfillment of the prophesies of Isaiah and Zechariah, they greeted Him as the answer to their hopes—the One they thought would restore their nation to them (Isaiah 62:11; Zechariah 9:9). They joyously welcomed Him with the messianic greeting from Psalm 118:25–26, "O

LORD, do save us. . . . . Blessed is the one who comes in the name of the LORD."

In fact, Christ made His triumphal entry into Jerusalem *on the very day* God had prophesied through Daniel that He would (Daniel 9:25–26). It is no wonder that the people greeted Jesus with shouts of "Hosanna to the Son of David" (Matthew 21:9). Hosanna means "Lord save us." The people in Jerusalem recognized Jesus as the heir of King David—the One who would free them from oppression. They recognized that the Messiah—the One they'd hoped for all their lives—had finally arrived.

Sadly, just a few days later, those crowds would disperse. The cross would shock them, make them question everything they believed, and leave them completely disheartened. With Jesus in the grave, and their hopes buried with Him, they went away devastated because they didn't really understand God's purposes. It was not until three days later, when Jesus rose from the dead, that they would see that the Lord had an even greater plan than they had imagined.

God did not act the way they thought He would. And He will not act as you expect either. Always remember this when opportunities—things you praised God for—seem to be destroyed. Always recall this

God did not act the way they thought He would. And He will not act as you expect either.

when you have your own cross to bear. Jesus said in Matthew 16:24, "If anyone wants to come after Me, he must deny himself, take up his cross, and follow Me." Do not give up because the sacrifices seem overwhelming or the path gets difficult. Do not despair when it seems as if your hopes have died. God has a greater plan and something better for you. Continue to trust your Savior regardless of how things appear. He has a way of resurrecting your dreams in a manner far beyond your imagination that is bound to make you truly joyful.

4

LIFTED UP

Jesus answered them by saying, "The hour has come for the Son of Man to be glorified. . . . Now My soul has become troubled; and what am I to say? 'Father, save Me from this hour'? But for this purpose I came to this hour. Father, glorify Your name." Then a voice came out of heaven: "I have both glorified it, and will glorify it again." So the crowd who stood by and heard it were saying that it had thundered; others were saying, "An angel has spoken to Him!" Jesus responded and said, "This voice has not come for My sake, but for yours. Now judgment is upon this world; now the ruler of this world will be cast out. And I, if I am lifted up from the earth, will draw all people to Myself." Now He was saying this to indicate what kind of death He was going to die.

JOHN 12:23, 27–33

*I*t is human nature to strive to be successful and recognized for our creativity, good looks, wisdom, strength, and talents. So being *glorified* and *lifted up* sounded great; that is, until the disciples realized that Jesus was signifying what kind of death He was going to die (John 12:33). As we saw in the previous chapter, they had hoped that He—as the Messiah—would inaugurate a powerful earthly kingdom. Some of the disciples also hoped they would rule with Him (Mark 10:35–37). However, all His talk of death quickly dashed their hopes.

What was even more confusing was that when Jesus had spoken about being *lifted up* earlier in their journey with Him, He had explained that it would be "as Moses lifted up the serpent in the wilderness" (John 3:14). That called to mind the well-known and terrible episode in Israel's history (Numbers 21:1–9).

The incident Jesus spoke of occurred right after God had given the Israelites victory over the Canaanites at Hormah. Though they had triumphed over their enemies, the Israelites were depressed and complaining. They were disheartened because instead of heading forward to the promised land, it looked as though they were headed backward—back to the Red Sea, where they had narrowly escaped the Egyptian army.

God was leading them around the enemy territory of Edom, but they didn't care. All they knew was that they were tired, and it felt as if this journey in the wilderness would never end. Why was the Lord doing this? In their discouragement, they "spoke against God and Moses: 'Why have you brought us up from Egypt to die in the wilderness? For there is no food and no water, and we are disgusted with this miserable food'" (Numbers 21:5).

It was unthinkable that the people who had been saved out of Egypt by the Lord's mighty hand would address Him and His servant Moses in such an ungrateful manner. And God's anger burned against them. He sent fiery serpents to bite the people, and many of them did not survive. This frightful plague of snakes lasted until they were willing to repent (Numbers 21:7). Then, in His mercy, "the LORD said to Moses, 'Make a fiery serpent, and put it on a flag pole; and it shall come about, that everyone who is bitten, and looks at it, will live'" (Numbers 21:8).

Understand this: As long as the fiery snakes were under the people's feet, they were deadly. However, as soon as Moses lifted one up and the people looked upon it, God made it the catalyst for their healing.

The same is true for your relationship with Jesus. As long as you hold Jesus under your feet—in the sense that you don't believe in Him because of your pride or limited vision—your own actions will condemn you (1 Peter 2:6–8). However, when you lift Christ up— honoring what He did for you on the cross—you will be healed.

In John 12, Jesus taught this important lesson to the disciples. He knew that they would be tempted by discouragement after the crucifixion, and He wanted them to understand that His death on the cross was the beginning of the true victory; that being *lifted up*—even in this excruciating manner—was the way all peoples would be saved (v. 32). Even though the disciples' goals of participating in an earthly kingdom were destroyed, Christ was showing them that they would inherit a better kingdom in heaven.

It can be difficult to remain faithful when your circumstances seem to be taking you away from your goals instead of toward them. However, don't make the mistake the Israelites did by speaking against God. Such faithless actions dishonor the Lord and hurt your spirit. They reveal that your heart is not right. They also demonstrate

When you lift Christ up—
honoring what He did for
you on the cross—you will
be healed.

that you are looking down on your circumstances instead of up to Jesus.

Instead of allowing your situation to defeat you, when you feel weary and disheartened, look to Christ—lift Him up in your life and praise Him. He knows your journey is long and difficult and that your heart can handle only so much (Psalm 103:14). Yet, surely, even the "backward" steps you're taking are leading you to a better goal. As long as you're looking to Jesus, He'll give you the strength and encouragement you need to carry on (Matthew 11:28–30). And the best thing about His plan is that along the way, as He's exalted in you, others will be saved as well.

5

A NEW COVENANT OF CONFIDENCE

When the hour came, He reclined at the table, and the apostles with Him. . . . When He had taken some bread and given thanks, He broke it and gave it to them, saying, "This is My body, which is being given for you; do this in remembrance of Me." And in the same way He took the cup after they had eaten, saying, "This cup, which is poured out for you, is the new covenant in My blood."

LUKE 22:14, 19–20

Considering that we have an all-knowing, all-powerful, always-present God as our Deliverer—One who is both able and *willing* to help us in any situation—why is it that we worry? Why would we do so? Ultimately, our problem finds its root in that we not only forget who we are but—even worse—we fail to remember who God is. We neglect to consider who we are in Him and what He has promised to us.

Because such forgetfulness is human nature, right before He went to the cross, Jesus had one last supper with the disciples. Christ realized that when His followers saw Him beaten, suspended on a cross, and buried in the tomb, they would be overcome with fear. So He took one more opportunity before His crucifixion to teach what He was going to accomplish for us all. During that historic meal, He gave them a visual illustration of what He was doing for them—so that whenever they would break bread, which was a daily occurrence, they would remember the salvation He provided. He knew they would need such a reminder in the days ahead. And that we would too.

In Luke 22:14–20, we read that Jesus met with His disciples in the upper room, and He said, "I have eagerly desired to eat this Passover with you before I suffer" (v. 15). Even though He had taught them about His path to the cross on several occasions (Matthew 12:40; 16:21; 17:22–23; 20:18–19), they didn't know what He was talking about. What they did know was that the Passover commemorated the deliverance of Israel from Egypt.

When the Hebrew people were hopelessly enslaved by the Egyptians, God had saved them in a miraculous manner—sending Moses to lead them and ten devastating plagues to set them free of Pharaoh's grasp. During the final plague, God said, "I will go through the land of Egypt on that night, and fatally strike all the firstborn in the land of Egypt, from the human firstborn to animals; and against all the gods of Egypt I will execute judgments—I am the LORD" (Exodus 12:12). However, to ensure that the people of Israel would remain safe, He said, "They shall take some of the blood and put it on the two doorposts and on the lintel of the houses. . . . The blood shall be a sign for you on the houses where you live; and when I see the blood I will pass over you, and no plague will come upon you to destroy you when I strike the land of Egypt" (Exodus 12:7, 13). Therefore, the Passover became a reminder of God's protection and deliverance. They remembered how the Lord liberated them through the blood of the lambs on their doorposts.

The Passover became a reminder of God's protection and deliverance—how the Lord liberated them through the blood of the lambs on their doorposts.

But then, centuries later, Jesus took a cup and said, "This cup, which is poured out for you, is the new covenant in My blood" (Luke 22:20). Jesus' blood? New covenant? The disciples knew about the old covenant, which God established after He freed the Israelites from Egypt by giving them the law of Moses (Exodus 19:5–24:7). But what of this new covenant? And what did it have to do with Jesus' blood?

For us today, it might help us to understand how two people would enter a covenant relationship in Jesus' day. It was a very serious commitment. The two parties would meet and exchange cloaks, which was their way of saying, "All that I have now belongs to you. What I own, you now own; and what you own, I now own. We are one." Then they would exchange weapons. In this way they were saying, "My strength is yours and your strength is mine. This is my commitment to you that if you need protection, I am available." Then they would cut their wrists and join them at the cut so their blood would intermingle, thus becoming one in their covenant relationship. Their scars served notice on would-be aggressors that they each had a "blood brother" who would come to their defense. Also, they adopted a part of each other's names.

Then, the covenant would be ratified by cutting an animal in half and separating it. The two parties would make a figure eight through and around the two parts. As they did this, they would make their oath or covenant, pledging their faithfulness and their support of each other. The two parties would decide what blessings and curses would come on the other as a result of keeping or failing to observe the covenant. Then they would pile stones together and at times would inscribe the conditions of the covenant on one of the stones— all to serve as a reminder of their pledge to each other.

Finally, the two would eat a simple meal together: a piece of bread that they would exchange. In this way they would be saying, "Here is what I am, and as you eat this, I am coming into you; I am becoming a part of you." They would exchange their cups of wine, again signifying that they would exchange their lives for each other; and thus, in all of this, demonstrating that whatever affects one affects the other. When one has need, the other responds. When one is under fire, the other is responsible to come to his or her defense. It was a binding blood covenant, joining the two parties in a relationship that would last for a lifetime.

This was the commitment Jesus was making with us as He sat

with the disciples at the Last Supper. Luke 22:19–20 tells us, "When He had taken some bread and given thanks, He broke it and gave it to them, saying, 'This is My body, which is being given for you; do this in remembrance of Me.' And in the same way He took the cup after they had eaten, saying, 'This cup, which is poured out for you, is the new covenant in My blood.'" Notice Jesus didn't say, "*our* blood" or "*your* blood." He said, "*My* blood."

This is significant because if you recall in chapter 1, "From the Beginning," we discussed how the sacrificial system given through the law of Moses was only provisional and imperfect; it couldn't save us. It was a temporary measure to atone for—or cover over—our sins until the Lord could implement His great plan. We could not give anything—not the blood of animal sacrifices or even our own blood—to make ourselves right with the Lord. But now, almighty God was ready to enter into a new covenant relationship with all mankind. And because it was wholly based on Jesus' body and blood, He was taking the full responsibility for the fulfillment of the new relationship. Our responsibility would be to accept it and live in gratefulness for what He has done for us.

This is what the Lord meant when He said this through the prophet Jeremiah:

> "Behold, days are coming," declares the LORD, "when *I will make* a new covenant with the house of Israel and the house of Judah, not like the covenant which I made with their fathers on the day I took them by the hand to bring them out of the land of Egypt, My covenant which they broke. . . . For this is the covenant which *I will make* with the house of Israel after those days," declares the LORD: "*I will* put My law within them and write it on their heart; and *I will* be their God, and they shall be My people. They will not teach again, each one his neighbor and each one his brother, saying, 'Know the LORD,' for they will all know Me, from the least of them to the greatest of them," declares the LORD, "for *I will* forgive their wrongdoing, and their sin I will no longer remember." (Jeremiah 31:31–34, emphasis added)

Notice the many times God says *He will* provide the new covenant for us. We could not pay the price of this new relationship, so Jesus paid it for us with His blood. Just as the lambs' blood on the doorposts protected and delivered Israel from Egypt, Jesus' blood—the blood of the Lamb of God—would save us from our sins.

This new relationship with God you and I have is an eternity-long commitment He has made to us—He is committed to being our peace, our provision, our protection, and our Guide.

And just like the covenants of His day, Jesus is saying to us, "All that I have now belongs to you. What I own, you now own." Or as He promises in Philippians 4:19, "My God will supply all your needs according to His riches in glory in Christ Jesus."

Christ is also saying, "My strength is yours. This is My commitment to you that when you need protection, I am available." Or as He assures in Isaiah 41:10, "Do not fear, for I am with you; do not be afraid, for I am your God. I will strengthen you, I will also help you, I will also uphold you with My righteous right hand."

This new relationship with God you and I have is an eternity-long commitment He has made to us—irrevocable, unchanging, everlasting, and unalterable. We have become a part of His family forever, and He is committed to being our peace, our provision, our protection, and our Guide. When you have Christ, you have everything.

So why should we ever worry? Certainly, there is no good reason. As Psalm 118:5–7 (NLT) says, "In my distress I prayed to the LORD, and the LORD answered me and set me free. The LORD is for me, so I will have no fear. What can mere people do to me? Yes, the LORD is for me; he will help me."

Friend, don't forget who you are and what Jesus has done for you. The God of this universe cares about you and will help you. "Therefore let's approach the throne of grace with confidence, so that we may receive mercy and find grace for help at the time of our need" (Hebrews 4:16).

The next time you sit to eat a piece of bread, remember His body was given for you. And the next time you take up a cup, think about Jesus' blood, which provides for your salvation and protection. Do it in remembrance of Him, and take heart that He will never let you down.

6

HE KNOWS YOUR DESPAIR

Then Jesus came with them to a place called Gethsemane, and told His disciples, "Sit here while I go over there and pray." And He took Peter and the two sons of Zebedee with Him, and began to be grieved and distressed. Then He said to them, "My soul is deeply grieved, to the point of death; remain here and keep watch with Me." And He went a little beyond them, and fell on His face and prayed, saying, "My Father, if it is possible, let this cup pass from Me; yet not as I will, but as You will."

MATTHEW 26:36–39

*J*esus knows exactly how you feel when you are at your low-est. When your circumstances appear unfair, your emotions are raw, and your pain is great, but you have no choice but to keep on. When you are already exhausted, but you must face the over-whelming challenges ahead of you. When those who should have supported you have abandoned and even betrayed you. When you've sacrificed all you can, and no one seems to appreciate it—and there is so much more you must do. When you are sleepless and all you can do is cry out, "God, please help me!" He understands. Even at this very moment, the struggles you face are not foreign to Him in the least. Indeed, your pain is very personal to Him.

After having dinner with the disciples and telling them about the new covenant He would purchase for us by His blood, the Lord Jesus went to a place called Gethsemane to pray before He went to the cross. There, He faced the enormity of the task before Him and the incredible physical, emotional, and spiritual agony He was about to feel. No doubt He considered the pain of being beaten and nailed to the cross, but that was not the greatest anguish He would face. Certainly, He had to think about no longer being physically pres-ent with the disciples and all the people who needed Him to heal,

We can and should go
often to the Father's arms
for compassion, mercy,
and consolation.

comfort, teach, and lead them. He must have thought of all the souls who would fail to accept His gracious gift and the eternal torment they would endure. And, of course, He had to consider the cost of bearing our sins, becoming sin itself, and overcoming the grave, and the toll that would take. It was a time of such profound desperation at Gethsemane that He said, "My soul is deeply grieved, to the point of death" (Matthew 26:38).

Scripture tells us that Jesus did not only pray once or twice—but He sought the Father three times during that terrible hour. If the perfect, sinless Son of the living God—God Himself—went repeatedly to the throne of grace for comfort as He faced such devastating emotions, what does that say to us? Not only are those feelings a reality for all of us, but we can and should go often to the Father's arms for compassion, mercy, and consolation.

Rejection, betrayal, loss, grief, physical pain—friend, your Savior has experienced them all. And when you face them, He feels great compassion for you (Matthew 9:36). Indeed, Gethsemane proves your Savior understands what it's like to be in so much agony that all you can do is weep and pray.

Jesus realizes how deep your feelings go and exactly what you need to survive the trials you face. In fact, He suffered just so He could fully comprehend your pain. Hebrews 2:17–18 (NLT) explains, "It was necessary for him to be made in every respect like us, his brothers and sisters, so that he could be our merciful and faithful High Priest before God. Then he could offer a sacrifice that would take away the sins of the people. Since he himself has gone through suffering and testing, he is able to help us when we are being tested."

In other words, Jesus not only knows your despair; He knows how to lead you triumphantly through it. So trust Him, obey Him, and hold on to the fact that He's with you, He cares about you, and He can minister to your hurting heart. And go to Him as often as you need. But also take His example and don't leave His presence until you're able to say, "Not as I will, but as You will." He will not only show you what to do, but He will give you the strength, wisdom, and comfort to endure it successfully. Indeed, "overwhelming victory is ours through Christ, who loved us" (Romans 8:37 NLT).

7

FOCUS IN TRIAL

All the chief priests and the elders of the people conferred together against Jesus to put Him to death; and they bound Him and led Him away, and handed Him over to Pilate the governor. . . . Now Jesus stood before the governor, and the governor questioned Him, saying, "So You are the King of the Jews?" And Jesus said to him, "It is as you say." And while He was being accused by the chief priests and elders, He did not offer any answer. Then Pilate said to Him, "Do You not hear how many things they are testifying against You?" And still He did not answer him in regard to even a single charge, so the governor was greatly amazed.

MATTHEW 27:1–2, 11–14

*T*here is no doubt that as Jesus stood trial in front of Pilate, He was completely focused. Matthew 27:12 tells us, "while He was being accused by the chief priests and elders, He did not offer any answer." Think about that. As the false accusations were being flung at Him, the Son of God didn't call a battalion of angels to His aid. He did not curse the priests and elders. He did not do anything to defend Himself. He did not answer.

However, it is important for us to understand *why* Christ didn't defend Himself: He had a much more important battle to fight, and He was not about to be distracted. In fact, He was about to engage in the war of the ages—the ultimate confrontation between sin and the holiness of God; death and eternal life.

Hebrews 12:2 helps us understand Christ's mindset: "Jesus, the originator and perfecter of the faith, who for the joy set before Him endured the cross, despising the shame." Jesus persevered through it all for "the joy set before Him." It was enough to stop Him from answering His accusers. It was sufficient to keep Him focused.

What was this overwhelming joy? Of course, it was doing the Father's will. However, it was also *you*. Galatians 2:20 says, "The Son of God . . . loved me and gave Himself up for me." Christ's joy was bringing you back to life and back into relationship with Him.

In other words, Jesus ignored His accusers' empty words because He was focused on what was immensely more crucial to Him, which was obeying the Father and saving you—that was His ultimate joy. It was far more important to Him to reconcile you to God than to vindicate Himself. Likewise, the Savior understood that just three days later, the Father would make the ultimate statement by raising Him from the grave. Not only would the resurrection silence Pilate and the religious leaders for good, but it would herald once and for all His everlasting victory over sin and death.

The point is, however, that you shouldn't underestimate the love Jesus has for you. True love gives itself sacrificially.

Perhaps you are feeling somewhat lonely or unloved today. Maybe you are wondering if anyone is thinking about you, wanting to express his or her deep care for your well-being. The answer is yes: Jesus is. He's thinking about you today, and He thought about you back then. He pictured you as He stood trial, and His love for you kept Him focused on the goal: to reconcile you to God. To show you His love—eternally.

So today, remember that you are Christ's joy—His beloved. He has given everything to show you His love, so be faithful to love Him in return. He focused on you; now you focus on Him.

The ENCOURAGING
MESSAGE *of the*
CROSS

*J*esus' sacrifice on the cross is the greatest gift ever given. It is God's grace at its zenith—the one moment on which the eternity of humankind hinges. It is freely given by God, and all He asks is that you believe it with all your heart.

8

THE WHY OF
THE CROSS

*They stripped [Jesus] and put a red cloak on Him. And after twisting together
a crown of thorns, they put it on His head, and put a reed in His right hand;
and they knelt down before Him and mocked Him, saying, "Hail, King of
the Jews!" And they spit on Him, and took the reed and beat Him on the
head. And after they had mocked Him, they took the cloak off Him and put
His own garments back on Him, and led Him away to crucify Him. . . .
And when they had crucified Him, they divided His garments among
themselves by casting lots. And sitting down, they began to keep watch
over Him there. And above His head they put up the charge against Him
which read, "THIS IS JESUS THE KING OF THE JEWS."*
MATTHEW 27:28–31, 35–37

We know Jesus faced the cross because He loves us. Yet when we consider *why* Jesus chose to endure the crucifixion for us, it is most likely the kind of dedication that is beyond what we can comprehend. After all, Jesus—God Himself—left His exalted position in heaven, where creation served as His footstool, and He "emptied Himself by taking the form of a bond-servant and being born in the likeness of men. And being found in appearance as a man, He humbled Himself by becoming obedient to the point of death: death on a cross" (Philippians 2:7–8). He was stripped naked, humiliated, mocked, beaten—made to suffer in every way a person can be debased. His nation rejected Him. His disciples deserted Him. Even Peter, one of His most intimate friends, denied Him.

And then there is the cross, which was an especially brutal way to die. His executioners stretched Jesus out on the rough-hewn wood, drove spikes through His hands and His feet. Then, after they'd hoisted Him up on the cross as a warning to others, He slowly suffocated to death. Every time He wanted to take a breath, He had to push Himself up by His only point of leverage—the nails in His feet, which tore at His flesh, nerves, and muscles. Most likely, His flogging-torn back scraped against the splintered wood and the crown of thorns dug deeper into His skull each time He attempted to fill His lungs with air. Just imagine the pain.

Meanwhile, the crowd yelled obscenities and ridiculed Him.

"If You are the Son of God, come down from the cross" (Matthew 27:40).

"He saved others; He cannot save Himself! He is the King of Israel; let Him now come down from the cross, and we will believe in Him" (Matthew 27:42).

"He has trusted in God; let God rescue Him now, if He takes pleasure in Him; for He said, 'I am the Son of God'" (Matthew 27:43).

And those were the religious people, who were supposed to serve God! They attacked Christ's identity, His ability to save, and worst of all, His relationship with the Father. The excruciating pain, heat, anger, betrayal, and frustration would have gotten the best of any of us. And as God, He could have had the entire host of heaven come to defend Him, pouring out His wrath and showing those sinful mockers who He really was. Maybe we would have been tempted, but not Jesus. His mission to save us was too important.

The pinnacle of Jesus' rejection, however, was when God the

"I came so that they would have life, and have it abundantly. I am the good shepherd; the good shepherd lays down His life for the sheep" (John 10:10–11).

Father, with whom Christ enjoyed perfect oneness, heaped all the sin of humankind onto His Son. In that agonizing moment on the cross, Jesus Christ bore the weight of every offense ever committed.

Certainly, the cross is the place in history where the greatest act of voluntary, sacrificial suffering and supreme love were demonstrated. True, Jesus never saw Himself as a victim of men and their evil desires. Instead, He viewed the cross as an opportunity to perform the Father's perfect will and to help us. In fact, He said, "I came so that they would have life, and have it abundantly. I am the good shepherd; the good shepherd lays down His life for the sheep. . . . I lay down My life so that I may take it back. No one has taken it away from Me, but I lay it down on My own. I have authority to lay it down, and I have authority to take it back. This commandment I received from My Father" (John 10:10–11, 17–18). Jesus went to His death on that terrible hill of Golgotha of His own volition. And instead of saving Himself, Jesus offered Himself as a living sacrifice—an expression of supreme love for you and me.

But why? Why was all that necessary? Yes, it was because of our sin. Isaiah explained, "He was pierced for our offenses, He was crushed for our wrongdoings; the punishment for our well-being was laid upon Him, and by His wounds we are healed" (Isaiah 53:5). But what actually happened on the cross that heals us?

Throughout the entire Old Testament, God's prophets preached this same message: redemption comes by supreme sacrifice. Every unblemished lamb that was slain for the Israelites' sin was a foreshadowing of Christ's substitutionary, sacrificial death. Even John the Baptist identified Jesus as man's sin-bearer, saying, "Behold, the Lamb of God who takes away the sin of the world!" (John 1:29). He knew Jesus was the last Lamb to come—the Lamb of God, the final sacrifice. When Christ died that day on the cross, eternal redemption was completed for us.

Yet many of us may wonder, "Why couldn't God simply say, 'You're forgiven'?" The reason is that His holiness demands a penalty be levied for sin—His righteousness demands payment. The Lord cannot act against His character and remain God. To overlook any sin, even one, is to act in opposition to His nature—and He is the Author of the moral code of the universe. The Lord says that our iniquity is so wicked, so vile, so destructive that in His holy, righteous, perfect mind, the only thing that can compensate for sin is death—the very penalty we have been given (Genesis 2:17; 3:19). And since each of us has violated the law, we cannot provide the payment for our own sin.

Without Jesus—the sinless Son of God—taking that penalty for us, we are left absolutely guilty and totally helpless. That means we are on track for wrath and separation from the Lord forever. And that is billions of times more painful, lonely, depressing, and humiliating than our very worst days here on earth.

Christ chose to pay the hefty cost. Colossians 2:13–14 explains, "When you were dead in your wrongdoings and the uncircumcision of your flesh, [Jesus] made you alive together with Him, having forgiven us all our wrongdoings, having canceled the certificate of debt consisting of decrees against us, which was hostile to us; and He has taken it out of the way, having nailed it to the cross."

Thankfully, God's offer of salvation is for anyone who willingly believes in His Son, the Lord Jesus Christ (John 3:16–18, 36; 2 Peter 3:9). Jesus came with that mission in mind, and He endured the cross to make that payment for us.

So the next time you think God owes you anything, think about this: your eternal destiny was set at the garden of Eden—an eternal death, separated from the Lord forever (Ephesians 2:1–3). Yet because of His everlasting, unconditional love for you and in His infinite mercy and grace, God's only Son bridged the gap for you to have eternal life through the cross. Forgiveness of sin, reconciliation with the Father, and the gift of eternal and abundant life were all made possible through Christ's atoning death.

Therefore, instead of thinking about what you don't have, consider all He has provided for you already. Set your heart to worship Jesus for the way He gave Himself for you. And trust Him. After all, "He who did not spare His own Son, but delivered Him over for us all, how will He not also with Him freely give us all things?" (Romans 8:32).

6

FORSAKEN FOR YOU

From the sixth hour darkness fell upon all the land until the ninth hour. And about the ninth hour Jesus cried out with a loud voice, saying, "ELI, ELI, LEMA SABAKTANEI?" that is, "MY GOD, MY GOD, WHY HAVE YOU FORSAKEN ME?" . . .

Jesus cried out again with a loud voice, and gave up His spirit. And behold, the veil of the temple was torn in two from top to bottom.

MATTHEW 27:45–46, 50–51

*M*e have all at least thought it: *My God, why have You forsaken me?* We've all come to the point where we feel as though the Lord has left us to despair in our bad situations. Whether it's because of medical problems, relational difficulties, or financial setbacks—we know what it's like to feel abandoned.

Yet, for some reason, it's disturbing that Jesus said it on the cross. Matthew 27:46 tells us, "About the ninth hour Jesus cried out with a loud voice, saying, 'ELI, ELI, LEMA SABACHTANI?' that is, 'MY GOD, MY GOD, WHY HAVE YOU FORSAKEN ME?'"

The word *forsaken* means "to abandon" or "to leave helpless." Yet, generally, we are accustomed to hearing it in terms of the Father's promise to never desert us. As Deuteronomy 31:6 says, "The LORD your God, He is the One who goes with you. He will not leave you nor forsake you" (NKJV).

Therefore, because we know that the Father honors His promises, we are convinced that He is never going to abandon us. And even when it feels as if God is nowhere to be found, we claim the promise and have confidence that He is still with us.

However, when we read that Jesus said it on the cross, it's some-what disconcerting. Of course, we understand that Christ had to be crucified in order to forgive us of our sins (Hebrews 9:22), and we know that it was excruciating for Him. We also know that He was quoting Psalm 22:1, a lament by David that pointed toward the Messiah. Still, it was an outburst that seems strange coming from Jesus.

Think about it: Jesus had already been on the cross almost six hours. Why did He say it just as He was about to die—when He was almost through with the mission? After all, Jesus knew that the Father would keep His promise to resurrect Him from the grave (Psalm 16:10). So, knowing the promise, and understanding the suffering would be over very soon—why did Jesus say that God had forsaken Him? We know it couldn't be from a lack of faith.

Sometimes in the immensity of all that happened at the cross, we lose the beautiful details of God's astounding plan. However, it's important to note the exact moment when Jesus cried out. The Mishnah, which is the oral law of the Jewish people, reports, "The slaughter of the Passover Lamb was performed during the ninth hour." The ninth hour. We learn that at the exact moment when the lambs were being sacrificed in the temple, Jesus was crying out about being forsaken.

At the exact moment
when the lambs were being
sacrificed in the temple,
Jesus was crying out about
being forsaken.

If you've ever wondered when exactly Jesus became our sin offering—understand that it was in that one awful, horrifying, redeeming moment that He cried out. Because it was in that moment that He became sin for us. As Paul teaches us in 2 Corinthians 5:21, "He made Him who knew no sin to be sin in our behalf, so that we might become the righteousness of God in Him." In 1 Corinthians 5:7 Paul confirmed, "Indeed Christ, our Passover, was sacrificed for us" (NKJV).

In that moment, Jesus knew what it meant to be separated from God. For the first time since before the beginning of time, Jesus didn't feel the Father's presence. That doesn't mean the Godhead was breached—Jesus was still fully God. Rather, it means that the Son understood the poverty of being separated from the Father. The hopelessness of it. The loneliness of it. It was the most heart-wrenching, awful moment of His life—worse than any scourging, beating, or crucifixion.

Perhaps that was the way Jesus best experienced what it's like to be us—what it feels like to be a sinner—without actually being one (Hebrews 2:14).

In that moment, Jesus felt every fear that you and I feel. He felt the consequences of sin. He felt what it means to be forsaken—what it means to be without God's perfect love. Maybe that's what is at the core of every time we feel forsaken, abandoned, enraged, offended, and hurt: it all comes from fear. We're afraid of being left with nothing. We're scared of being unloved and rejected. We're terrified of dying alone. However, at the core of it all is the fear that comes from not feeling the Father's perfect love.

Yet 1 John 4:18 assures us, "There is no fear in love, but perfect love drives out fear, because fear involves punishment, and the one who fears is not perfected in love." Perfect love doesn't abandon you. When you experience God's unconditional love and are obedient to His will, it doesn't matter what happens—you are fully convinced of His provision and protection.

But if Jesus felt that separation from God, how can we know that *we* will never be forsaken by God? We can know it for certain because of what happened afterward. Matthew 27:50–51 reports, "Jesus cried out again with a loud voice, and gave up His spirit. And behold, the veil of the temple was torn in two from top to bottom."

The tearing of the temple veil may not seem like a meaningful detail to us today; however, it is utmost in significance to us spiritually.

Christ knows exactly how you feel. He knows the depth of your pain. And He did not leave you helpless.

This is because, historically, the veil of the temple separated every person from the most holy place—the holiest place in the temple, where God's presence was said to dwell. The Talmud reports that the veil was approximately four inches thick, sixty feet high, and required three hundred priests just to hang it or take it down. This, of course, was to prevent anyone from advancing into God's presence uninvited or getting a glimpse into that special chamber. Only the high priest was permitted to approach the Lord in the Most Holy Place; and he was only allowed to approach on one specific day of the year—the Day of Atonement.

But when the veil was split in two, it signified that Jesus had succeeded in removing *all* that separated us from the Father. Think about it: that immense, heavy, thick veil tore from *top* to bottom. It was removed from above. Only God could have rent it in that manner. And by doing so, the Lord was showing once and for all that *He* had removed the barrier between Him and us (2 Corinthians 3:16; Hebrews 6:19–20; 10:19–20). Through Jesus' death, He opened the way for all people to have direct access to His presence—always, at any moment.

Therefore, whenever you feel forsaken, remember that the

resurrected Christ knows exactly how you feel. He knows the depth of your pain. And He did not leave you helpless to face your fears—He did not abandon you to a life without the perfect love of God.

So the next time you read the profound words, "My God, My God, why have You forsaken Me?" thank Jesus for identifying with you in such a deep way. And realize that you can always count on Him, because there's no situation you will face that He will not face with you.

10

AS THE KING
HE IS

*Now when it was evening, a rich man from Arimathea came, named
Joseph, who himself had also become a disciple of Jesus. This man went to
Pilate and asked for the body of Jesus. Then Pilate ordered it to be given
to him. And Joseph took the body and wrapped it in a clean linen cloth,
and laid it in his own new tomb, which he had cut out in the rock; and
he rolled a large stone against the entrance of the tomb and went away.*

MATTHEW 27:57–60

*B*odies that had been crucified were not given the honor and dignity of a burial. Rather, they were flung out onto the city dung heap. It was the most humiliating and horrifying thing that could happen to a Jew—or anyone, for that matter. To be treated as refuse at death was the ultimate disgrace.

Had Jesus been the common criminal the religious leaders said He was, His pierced and broken body would have been defiled with the rest of the thieves and scoundrels. However, as the Messiah and the Son of the living God, Jesus was buried in the manner befitting His person.

John 19:38–42 shows us the loving care with which Joseph of Arimathea and Nicodemus treated Jesus' body.

Joseph of Arimathea, being a disciple of Jesus, but secretly, for fear of the Jews, asked Pilate that he might take away the body of Jesus; and Pilate gave him permission. So he came and took the body of Jesus. And Nicodemus, who at first came to Jesus by night, also came, bringing a mixture of myrrh and aloes, about a hundred pounds. Then they took the body of Jesus, and bound it in strips of linen with the spices, as the custom of the Jews is to bury. Now in the place where He was crucified there was a garden, and in the garden a new tomb in which no one had yet been laid. So there they laid Jesus, because of the Jews' Preparation Day, for the tomb was nearby. (NKJV)

Understand that when Joseph of Arimathea and Nicodemus treated Jesus with tenderness and respect in His burial, it was to fulfill prophecy. Psalm 16:10 promises, "You will not leave my soul in Sheol, nor will You allow Your Holy One to see corruption" (NKJV). God had promised that the Messiah would not suffer decay in the grave. And in faithfulness to His promise, God did not allow Jesus to be dishonored in His burial.

That's why Christ was buried in a tomb—and not just any tomb. Most burial chambers in Israel at the time had space for eight to thirteen people, but the tomb they put Jesus in was brand-new. It had just been cut out—there had never been a dead body there, which means that it had never been defiled by death. So the body of the Messiah never inhabited a place with decay.

Also, during a burial, the body was usually watched, washed, anointed with preparatory spices, and either wrapped with cloth or bound in burial shrouds that were made of strips of linen. The face was bound separately with a face cloth or just covered. The hundred

Everything surrounding the crucifixion and resurrection of Jesus Christ shows us how God keeps every one of His promises.

pounds of myrrh and aloes that Nicodemus brought were sufficient to treat between one hundred and two hundred bodies—though it was customary to give only monarchs and other highly respected officials that vast amount of spices. Jesus was treated like a king in every way.

God didn't only keep His Son from being treated like a criminal and put on the city trash heap. The Father didn't merely prevent Christ from seeing decay (Acts 2:31–32; 13:34–35, 37). Rather, even in death—however brief it was—the Lord showed our Savior the honor and dignity that was reserved for kings (Philippians 2:9–11)!

Everything surrounding the crucifixion and resurrection of Jesus Christ shows us how God keeps every one of His promises. For Christians, this is extremely important because even when we don't realize it, the Lord is keeping His promises to us in a way that goes above and beyond what we could ever imagine (Ephesians 3:20).

Therefore, trust Him. And honor Christ as King in your heart.

11

MOMENTS OF REFLECTION

It was a preparation day, and a Sabbath was about to begin.
Now the women who had come with [Jesus] from Galilee
followed, and they saw the tomb and how His body was laid.
And then they returned and prepared spices and perfumes. And
on the Sabbath they rested according to the commandment.

LUKE 23:54–56

*T*he quiet moments after a devastating loss are often the most heart-breaking. You take care of what needs to be done and attempt to process your thoughts and emotions—trying to understand what's happened to you. For Jesus' followers, that meant observing the Sabbath and the Passover. They kept doing what God had called them to do regardless of their circumstances.

But that means we know what Christ's disciples were doing from the moment they saw Jesus crucified to when they knew He had risen from the dead. Every element they experienced—the prayers, blessings, and rituals they were commanded to practice during these memorials—would have reminded them of Jesus. Indeed, just twenty-four hours earlier, they were dining with Him and He was teaching them about each facet of their observance.

Did they look at the cup of wine on the table and remember Him saying, "This is My blood of the covenant, which is being poured out for many for forgiveness of sins" (Matthew 26:28)? The night before, that statement had seemed strange, but now they had a new perspective. Now it was real. They had seen His blood pour from Him.

And as they blessed the matzo (unleavened bread) and it broke in the hands of the one saying the blessing, how could they help but

$\mathcal{I}$t was in remembering His words that they would find hope that this was not the end.

remember Jesus' words, "This is My body, which is being given for you; do this in remembrance of Me" (Luke 22:19)? They had certainly seen Him broken. Now, memories seemed to be all they had.

It had to be very painful. They had to be confused, to say the least.

Of course, from the foundation of the world, God knew this would happen. Why would He set it up this way? Why would the Lord give the disciples constant reminders of what Christ had taught them? He did so because of how important it is to keep focusing on Him when all hope seems lost. The time was absolutely filled with attention to Jesus—opportunities to think about all He said and what He had done for them. It was in remembering His words that they would find hope that this was not the end.

And what an incredible difference three days would make. Certainly, the disciples would find the wisdom of Psalm 30:5 to be true: "His anger is but for a moment, His favor is for a lifetime; weeping may last for the night, but a shout of joy comes in the morning."

Friend, it isn't in burying your feelings that you find meaning and triumph—it's in taking them to Jesus. He has promises for you to cling to and hope for your hurting soul. Even when you don't know how things will turn out, He will give you comfort, hope, and peace that transcends your understanding. "Did I not say to you that if you believe, you will see the glory of God?" (John 11:40).

THE POWER *of the* RESURRECTION *for* YOU

If uncertainties have smothered your confidence in the Lord, remember His power so evident in the empty tomb. The crucifixion was not the end of the story—and neither is the trial you face. Choose the path of faith, and declare that triumph lies just ahead. Allow His resurrection to strengthen your hope, renew your certainty, and be your greatest victory.

12

THE PLACE
OF MERCY

When the Sabbath was over, Mary Magdalene, Mary the mother of
James, and Salome bought spices so that they might come and anoint
Him. And very early on the first day of the week, they came to the
tomb. . . . Looking up, they noticed that the stone had been rolled away;
for it was extremely large. And entering the tomb, they saw a young
man sitting at the right, wearing a white robe; and they were amazed.
But he said to them, "Do not be amazed; you are looking for Jesus the
Nazarene, who has been crucified. He has risen; He is not here."

MARK 16:1–2, 4–6

*O*nce a year, on the Day of Atonement, the high priest would enter in behind the veil of the Most Holy Place and stand before God. On that day, he would sprinkle blood on the mercy seat in order to receive forgiveness for the sins of the community. It was there that the shekinah glory—or presence of God—would rest between the golden figures of two cherubim, which were a kind of angel.

As we saw in chapter 9, "Forsaken for You," only one man could be in the presence of God, and on only one day a year. One man, once a year—and by the time Jesus walked on the earth, it had been hundreds of years since the shekinah glory of God had been seen in the temple. The average Israelite was not accustomed to being in the presence of the Father.

Yet imagine the excitement and glory on the Day of Atonement when the Lord's presence would dwell between the two angels. In Exodus 25:22, God says, "There I will meet with you, and I will speak with you from above the mercy seat, from between the two cherubim which are on the ark of the Testimony, about everything which I will give you in commandment to the children of Israel" (NKJV).

It was there on the mercy seat—between the two angels, above the ark of the testimony—that God showed Himself merciful in forgiving sin. God met with the high priest and spoke with him. And the high priest had the privilege of worshiping God and finding guidance.

Now, fast-forward to three days after the crucifixion. It was very early in the morning, and Mary Magdalene and some other women had traveled to Jesus' tomb out of love and devotion. John 20:11–12 tells us, "Mary was standing outside the tomb, weeping; so as she wept, she stooped to look into the tomb; and she saw two angels in white sitting, one at the head and one at the feet, where the body of Jesus had been lying."

Though Mary did not realize it at the time, what she was seeing was the wondrous fulfillment of the Old Testament mercy seat—the glory of the Lord shone between those two angels. Only, God's shekinah glory was not being revealed to a priest with an offering; rather, it was being shown to a woman with a broken heart.

Why would God put the mercy seat in the tomb? The interesting thing is that the mercy seat was the cover of the ark of the testimony. The word for *ark* in the Hebrew is *arown*, which means "coffin." God's glory appeared in the Old Testament above a coffin. And now, through Christ, God's great victory had likewise appeared over the tomb—to signify His victory over death.

You see, Jesus had already become our High Priest, and He had already made our atonement offering (Hebrews 9:23–28). The veil of the Most Holy Place had been torn in two, and we were no longer separated from the presence of the Lord (Hebrews 10:19–23). The forgiveness, the guidance, and the very presence of God—that had previously been accessible to only one man on one day a year—had been made available to all of us for all eternity.

No matter what you've done, no matter what sin you've committed—the mercy seat is available for your forgiveness.

No matter what counsel you need, no matter why you need direction—the mercy seat is available to give you guidance.

No matter what the tomb, no matter what hope or promise has died to you—the mercy seat is available to you, and the glory of God will shine on your situation.

You may not see it yet, but the victory is yours. Jesus Christ has become your mercy seat—He has opened the way so that the shekinah glory of God can illuminate your life in every circumstance.

So what do you do with this great access to the mercy seat?

Hebrews 4:16 says, "Let's approach the throne of grace with confidence, so that we may receive mercy and find grace for help at the time of our need."

Therefore, enter in, friend, and rejoice in the glory of God.

13

ENCOURAGEMENT FROM THE EMPTY TOMB

Peter and the other disciple left, and they were going to the tomb. . . .
He entered the tomb; and he looked at the linen wrappings lying there,
and the face-cloth which had been on His head, not lying with the linen
wrappings but folded up in a place by itself. So the other disciple who had
first come to the tomb also entered then, and he saw and believed. For they
did not yet understand the Scripture, that He must rise from the dead.

JOHN 20:3, 6–9

*t*here's no question that the disciples who followed Jesus fully trusted that He was the Savior. They truly believed that their leader and teacher was the Messiah. But as we've discussed, after Christ's crucifixion, they struggled with disappointment and disbelief because of some of the mistaken notions they had of His mission. The disciples had watched as His lifeless body was taken down off the cross, and their hope appeared absolutely lost. A dead man could not possibly save them or deliver Israel—no matter how wonderful He was or how powerful His promises sounded.

Imagine for a moment how brokenhearted, fearful, and disillusioned those faithful men must have been. Perhaps their heartbreak is easy for you to understand because you've also experienced terrible loss. You realize what it is like to feel pain and confusion, unsure of which way to turn or what is going to happen. You need encouragement and the assurance that everything is going to be all right.

But when we think about the cross, you and I should recall that the disciples' lives were changed the moment they looked into the tomb. Scripture tells us, "Peter got up and ran to the tomb; and when he stooped and looked in, he saw the linen wrappings only; and he went away to his home, *marveling at what had happened"* (Luke 24:12, emphasis added).

What Jesus had promised was true! The tomb was empty! Christ had risen from the dead!

What an awesome truth for us to cling to no matter what our situation or circumstance. When all seemed lost, Jesus Christ defeated death and rose victoriously from the grave. Likewise, He can lead you and me to triumph in every trial, regardless of how desperate things may appear initially.

This assurance should fill your heart with hope and joy today—it certainly does mine. In fact, during a performance of First Baptist Church of Atlanta's passion play several years ago, I got completely caught up by the awesomeness of the resurrection. My role was to step onstage at the end of the production and explain to the audience how to be saved through faith in Christ. So I stood behind the curtain, waited for my cue, and watched the gospel story unfold.

Well, when the scene at the empty tomb took place and the angel declared that Jesus had risen from the dead, I became so excited that I lunged onto the stage with the play still in progress! There I was, in my suit and tie, while everyone else was dressed in costumes from

The risen Savior is active on our behalf—leading, providing for, and defending us at every turn. And we could not have a better Champion.

biblical times. I couldn't help myself. My heart was so overjoyed that I just couldn't wait to look inside that empty tomb.

What is it that makes Christ's victory over the grave so encouraging? First, as we've seen, it gives us hope because Jesus is alive, seated at the Father's right hand, and looking out for you and me. The victorious Warrior who defeated sin and death is our Advocate. Hebrews 7:25 says, "He always lives to make intercession for [us]." We don't serve a prophet or leader who is dead and unable to help us in our time of need. The risen Savior is active on our behalf—leading, providing for, and defending us at every turn. And we could not have a better Champion.

Second, the empty tomb fills us with confidence because it is a guarantee of our eternal life. We have undeniable evidence that God keeps His promise of salvation to us. Romans 6:4–5 explains, "Christ was raised from the dead through the glory of the Father, so we too might walk in newness of life. For if we have become united with Him in the likeness of His death, certainly we shall also be in the likeness of His resurrection." Of course, most people take this to signify the promise of heaven—of having a home with God forever. And it does. Since Jesus lives, it is certain that we will as well—and so will all our loved ones who believe in Him. But it does not only mean that we will enjoy life *then*; rather, it means we have resurrection life *right now*.

John 17:3 says, "This is eternal life, that they may know You, the only true God, and Jesus Christ whom You have sent." Did you catch that? The very nature of our everlasting life is based on, fulfilled in, and characterized by our relationship with the Savior. This is because Jesus gives us a new quality to this life that is unlike anything we have ever known—a new dimension of being that is spiritually vivacious. His divine nature indwells and transforms us. And He does so through the presence of His Holy Spirit.

Jesus said, "The Helper, the Holy Spirit whom the Father will send in My name, He will teach you all things, and remind you of all that I said to you" (John 14:26). The Holy Spirit is the Lord's constant presence with us, indwelling us for the purpose of blessing, training, enabling, strengthening, energizing, equipping, guiding, healing, informing, transforming, warning, and producing eternal fruit through us. We enter a new plane of existence because the resurrected Savior establishes His own presence in us. This is why 2 Corinthians 5:17 instructs, "If anyone is in Christ, this person is a new creation; the old things passed away; behold, new things have come." We relinquish our imperfect and limited earthly existence so that we can gain Christ's powerful resurrection life that touches every aspect of our being (Philippians 3:10–11).

Finally, the empty tomb is so encouraging because we know that everything Jesus said to us is absolutely true. Our Savior kept His pledge to reconcile us to the Father; we know He can and will keep every other promise He has made to us. Romans 8:31–32 reminds us, "If God is for us, who is against us? He who did not spare His own Son, but delivered Him over for us all, how will He not also with Him freely give us all things?" There is nothing we could ever need or encounter that requires more power to overcome than what Jesus experienced on the cross and in the grave. No matter what you face, the Lord is able to help you through it. This is why Paul wrote these wonderful words to us in Ephesians 1:18–21 (NLT):

> I pray that your hearts will be flooded with light so that you can understand the confident hope he has given to those he called—his holy people who are his rich and glorious inheritance.
>
> I also pray that you will understand the incredible greatness of God's

power for us who believe him. This is the same mighty power that raised Christ from the dead and seated him in the place of honor at God's right hand in the heavenly realms. Now he is far above any ruler or authority or power or leader or anything else—not only in this world but also in the world to come.

So consider: Does your hope appear lost today? Have you had to carry your own cross—experiencing some trial or discouragement that has left you with heartache or pain? Are you struggling with confusion or uncertainty—not knowing which way to turn or what will happen to you or your loved ones?

If so, then look to the empty tomb, be encouraged, and find the assurance that everything is going to be all right. Your Savior is alive and interceding on your behalf, He has given you everything needed not only to survive but to triumph in your situation, and He has promised to help you. There is absolutely nothing in this world that should ever take away your joy and confidence in His perfect provision. So rejoice that He is your Defender, He's made you alive, and you will see His resurrection power demonstrated through whatever you face.

We relinquish our imperfect and limited earthly existence so that we can gain Christ's powerful resurrection life.

14

VICTORY THROUGH BELIEVING

Thomas, one of the twelve, who was called Didymus, was not with them when Jesus came. So the other disciples were saying to him, "We have seen the Lord!" But he said to them, "Unless I see in His hands the imprint of the nails, and put my finger into the place of the nails, and put my hand into His side, I will not believe." Eight days later His disciples were again inside, and Thomas was with them. Jesus came, the doors having been shut, and stood in their midst and said, "Peace be to you."

JOHN 20:24–26

homas was missing when Jesus first appeared to the disciples, and he was also the one to voice the greatest doubt about the resurrection. It had been eight days since the tomb was found empty, and many people had testified seeing the risen Savior, but that didn't make a difference to Thomas. He just didn't trust the reports and declared that he would not believe that Christ had risen from the grave unless he touched Jesus' hands and side (John 20:25). Perhaps you can appreciate his doubts. When we experience a terrible loss, sometimes it is difficult to believe that the Lord is working in the unseen.

After all, when it comes to earthly matters, we often learn the hard way that seeing is believing—that evidence is necessary when judging others' claims. So it can be quite a difficult switch when it comes to spiritual matters. We want to trust God, but the reality of our circumstances can crush our faith.

Still, Thomas had witnessed Jesus perform one miracle after another—healing the sick, restoring sight to the blind, casting out demons, multiplying loaves and fishes, and so much more. He knew what Christ could do. Certainly, it is understandable that Thomas might not have fully comprehended how Jesus would have victory over the grave. Undoubtedly, when he saw the Lord nailed to the cross and dying that terrible death, all his hopes were shattered. Sadly, however, Thomas did not trust all Christ said about the resurrection. And whenever we don't believe what God says, we are headed for trouble.

You can imagine the shock and embarrassment Thomas felt when Jesus appeared before him—offering His nail-pierced hands and riven side to Thomas for proof. "He said to Thomas, 'Place your finger here, and see My hands; and take your hand and put it into My side; and do not continue in disbelief, but be a believer.' Thomas answered and said to Him, 'My Lord and my God!' Jesus said to him, 'Because you have seen Me, have you now believed?'" (John 20:27–29).

What happened to Thomas can be instructive for you today— especially if God has made you a promise that you've waited a long time to see fulfilled. What you believe about His character and Scripture will ensure either your success or your failure.

You may, like Thomas, demand that the Lord show you signs, but when you do so, you only prove the weakness and immaturity of your faith.

The resurrection is all the
proof we need about what
God can and will do.

You see, the resurrection is really all the proof we need about what God can and will do (Romans 8:32). When the disciples finally realized that all Jesus had said was true and that He had risen from the dead after three days, it absolutely ignited them—their courage, their confidence, and their desire to tell the world the good news of salvation became unstoppable (Acts 5:28–32, 41–42). Thomas was so impassioned and empowered by seeing the risen Jesus that it is reported he took the gospel to Parthia and India.

Knowing what Jesus accomplished should fuel your faith as well. If you are a believer, you know that the resurrection is true, and it is your assurance that every promise Christ made to you will be perfectly fulfilled. With this in mind, it is important for you to view everything in your life through the reality of the resurrection—and *believe*. This doesn't mean you have confidence in a particular outcome; rather, it signifies that you trust God's provision and character, and you will keep following Him no matter how bad your situation looks or how dark the road becomes. You have faith that He will lead you through in the right way, in His timing.

You don't fear that He has rejected you or deemed you unworthy, because you have evidence that your sins have been permanently forgiven. He has accepted you, adopted you into His family, and given you a new identity (Romans 8:14–16). You have absolute proof that you've been given eternal life and a home in heaven—so there's nothing anyone can do to hurt you in any permanent way here (Psalm 118:4–8; Romans 6:8–10). You know you will not be alone on your journey because as your living Lord, He gives you His Holy Spirit to dwell in you, lead you, and empower you (John 14:16–20). You even have the comfort of knowing you will see your believing loved ones again when they pass away from this life (1 Thessalonians 4:14). So you trust that no matter what happens, Jesus is able and willing to lead you to victory.

Is there any situation in your life that demands more wisdom, love, and power than was displayed when Christ was raised from the dead? Don't embarrass yourself by doubting Him. Jesus said, "Blessed are they who did not see, and yet believed" (John 20:29). If you'll unwaveringly trust Him to do as He says, you will receive a great blessing. Not only will you see your dearest prayers answered, but you'll glorify Him and your faith will grow.

So whenever you encounter situations that seem impossible, always remember Jesus' victory over the grave and trust Him. Obey

God and leave all the consequences to Him, because He has promised to care for all of your needs as you follow Him. No doubt, through His resurrection power, your faith will be made sight. As the empty tomb shows—He is truly able!

15

THE NEXT MISSION

The eleven disciples proceeded to Galilee, to the mountain which Jesus had designated to them. And when they saw Him, they worshiped Him; but some were doubtful. And Jesus came up and spoke to them, saying, "All authority in heaven and on earth has been given to Me. Go, therefore, and make disciples of all the nations, baptizing them in the name of the Father and the Son and the Holy Spirit, teaching them to follow all that I commanded you; and behold, I am with you always, to the end of the age."

MATTHEW 28:16–20

*Y*ou can imagine that what Jesus said after He was raised from the dead was important. After all, He had a captive audience—people who realized all He had said was absolutely true and were most likely hanging on His every word. John 2:22 confirms, "When He had risen from the dead, His disciples remembered that He had said this to them; and they believed the Scripture and the word which Jesus had said" (NKJV).

So Jesus took the opportunity and gave them an important mission—or what we know as the *Great Commission*. He said, "All authority in heaven and on earth has been given to Me. Go, therefore, and make disciples of all the nations, baptizing them in the name of the Father and the Son and the Holy Spirit, teaching them to follow all that I commanded you; and behold, I am with you always, to the end of the age" (Matthew 28:18–20).

Still, the disciples may not have understood the full significance of what had occurred through Christ's death and resurrection—and what was still happening *through them*. After all, how would these poor, uneducated men make disciples, baptize others, and teach them what Jesus said? They weren't trained. And going to *all* nations to do so? There was no way. They didn't have mass communication or the modern means of travel, as we do. Even with our resources, it's an enormous, challenging, and overwhelming task. But to them it must have sounded absolutely impossible.

Likewise, we may understand that this Great Commission is Christ's mandate to us as well, but we may not realize how the Father had planned to do this from the beginning. Thankfully, the Lord helps us grasp what He was accomplishing in a powerful way. You see, the crucifixion and resurrection were not the end. They were just the beginning of a new, awesome way God was working in the world.

As we've seen over the previous pages, during the Passover Feast, Jesus became our sacrificial Lamb on the cross (1 Corinthians 5:7). We can see the spiritual significance of what occurred because we know the Passover was originally celebrated to mark Israel's exodus out of Egypt and out of bondage, and Jesus' death on the cross liberated us from the enslavement to sin. But the next festivals the Jewish people celebrated—which began right after Passover and were included in what was considered the Passover season—marked when the Jewish people received God's law at Mount Sinai. In other words, the next feasts celebrated not only that they were free to be His people but that they had the instruction to do so. Sadly, we often miss the beauty of what the next couple of feasts teach us about what it means to be the church. So let's take a look at them.

It is interesting to note that the harvest started on the third day after Passover with the Feast of Firstfruits—*the same day Jesus rose from the grave.* This is significant because during Firstfruits, people brought offerings of barley—the first crop of the year—to the temple. When God accepted it, it meant He was promising to provide them with the rest of the harvest (Leviticus 23:9–14; Proverbs 3:9–10). In 1 Corinthians 15:20, Paul explained, "Christ has been raised from the dead. He is the first of a great harvest of all who have died" (NLT). In other words, because the Lord accepted Jesus' offering on the cross and He was resurrected from the dead, He is guaranteeing that all who believe in Him will as well.

But as we've noted, this was only the beginning. Jesus Himself said, "Truly I say to you, the one who believes in Me, the works that I do, he will do also; and greater works than these he will do; because I am going to the Father" (John 14:12). With this in view, after the resurrection, Jesus taught His disciples for forty days. Acts 1:3 explains, "During the forty days after he suffered and died, he appeared to the apostles from time to time, and he proved to them in many ways that

$\mathcal{B}$ecause the Lord accepted Jesus' offering on the cross and He was resurrected from the dead, He is guaranteeing that all who believe in Him will as well.

he was actually alive. And he talked to them about the Kingdom of God" (NLT).

For forty days, Jesus prepared them for the mission—for the disciples to be emissaries of His kingdom. But He did not send them off right away. Rather, "He commanded them not to leave Jerusalem, but to wait for what the Father had promised" (Acts 1:4). Soon thereafter, Jesus ascended to heaven, and for the next ten days, the disciples prayed.

This brings us to fifty days after the resurrection, which is the feast known as the Feast of Weeks or Pentecost—a festival that celebrated the harvest and God's provision of the law on Mount Sinai. But when this feast found its fulfillment through Jesus, the truly miraculous occurred.

Perhaps you've read Acts 2 and know of the amazing events that happened in Jerusalem that day. Verses 1–4 tell us:

When the day of Pentecost had come, [Jesus' followers] were all together in one place. And suddenly a noise like a violent rushing wind came from heaven, and it filled the whole house where they were sitting. And tongues that looked like fire appeared to them, distributing themselves, and a tongue rested on each one of them. And they were all filled with the Holy Spirit and began to speak with different tongues, as the Spirit was giving them the ability to speak out.

In that moment, the disciples received exactly what they would need to carry out the Great Commission that Jesus had commanded of them—the person of the Holy Spirit. We talked about this resurrection-empowered life that God gives us through His Holy Spirit in chapter 13, "Encouragement from the Empty Tomb." The Lord God lives *His life* through you, providing you with everything you need for all He assigns you to do. Notice what He gave to the disciples—He gave them the ability to speak out in different languages. Why would He do that?

Acts 2:5–6 tells us, "There were Jews residing in Jerusalem, devout men *from every nation under heaven.* And when this sound occurred, the crowd came together and they were bewildered, because each one of them was hearing them speak in his own language" (emphasis added). Those faithful Jews had gone to Jerusalem in obedience to the command to celebrate Pentecost (Deuteronomy 16:16), but God was preparing the field for them to take part in a different harvest—an

The Lord God lives His life through you, providing you with everything you need for all He assigns you to do.

eternal one. Those devout Jews began hearing the disciples speaking the gospel in their own languages! And how did the crowd respond?

> They were completely amazed. "How can this be?" they exclaimed. "These people are all from Galilee, and yet we hear them speaking in our own native languages! Here we are—Parthians, Medes, Elamites, people from Mesopotamia, Judea, Cappadocia, Pontus, the province of Asia, Phrygia, Pamphylia, Egypt, and the areas of Libya around Cyrene, visitors from Rome (both Jews and converts to Judaism), Cretans, and Arabs. And we all hear these people speaking in our own languages about the wonderful things God has done!" (Acts 2:7–11 NLT)

Those uneducated men who followed Jesus were suddenly empowered through the presence of the Holy Spirit to proclaim the good news of salvation in every language present. He was *within* them, teaching, empowering, and directing them so His plan could be fulfilled *through* them. Remember: Jesus had commanded His followers to make disciples of all nations, and He not only gave them the tools (languages) to reach them; He brought the nations *to them*. Acts 2:41 tells us, "Those who believed what Peter said were baptized and added to the church that day—about 3,000 in all" (NLT). On that day, the church was born. And on that day, Jesus showed us why "the one who believes in Me, the works that I do, he will do also; and greater works than these he will do" (John 14:12). We would do "greater works" because He would work through us as His body through the power and wisdom of His Holy Spirit. What an awesome Savior we serve!

If that doesn't excite your soul, I don't know what will!

And you, friend, have the magnificent privilege of being part of the ongoing Pentecost—the continuing harvest of souls for the kingdom of God. Of course, you may look at what happened in Acts 2 and think, *Wow, look at what Christ did through them.* But don't miss the fact that it is a pattern of how He wants to work through you. He may not provide you with the gift of languages, but He has certainly enabled you to serve Him in a powerful way through the spiritual gifts He gives you (Romans 12:4–8; 1 Corinthians 12; 1 Peter 4:10). Because the truth of the matter is that the power, provision, instruction, and equipping God gave the disciples is available to you. From the moment you accept Christ as your Savior, you are sealed with the Holy Spirit, who empowers you to do all the Lord plans for you to accomplish. So not only *can* you be part of God's great work, but you'll find true joy, fulfillment, and meaning in life when you walk in His purposes for you (Ephesians 2:10).

Jesus said, "The harvest is plentiful, but the workers are few. Therefore, plead with the Lord of the harvest to send out workers into His harvest" (Matthew 9:37–38). Friend, heed Christ's call and obey His instruction. You absolutely cannot go wrong trusting or serving Him. On the contrary, you'll be amazed at the truly miraculous things He will do.

16

RESURRECTION POWER TO LIVE BY NOW

Blessed be the God and Father of our Lord Jesus Christ, who according to His great mercy has caused us to be born again to a living hope through the resurrection of Jesus Christ from the dead, to obtain an inheritance which is imperishable, undefiled, and will not fade away, reserved in heaven for you.

1 Peter 1:3–4

We've taken this journey to the cross and seen that Jesus is the fulfillment of all God promised. And He is still accomplishing His mission to seek and save the lost through you, me, and other believers (Luke 19:10). The resurrection of Christ was more than a divine and miraculous event in the first century. It was the dawning of a new way, the birth of everlasting hope, and the confirmation that Jesus really is *Immanuel*—"God with us"—permanently (Matthew 1:23). The known world was never the same after the cross. And we shouldn't be either.

I realize that as you sit here reading this, there may be some personal cross you bear. Physical infirmities, relational difficulties, financial struggles, occupational challenges, political and social unrest, setbacks, disappointments, and losses of many kinds can overwhelm us to the point of hopelessness. Jesus said, "If anyone wants to come after Me, he must deny himself, take up his cross, and follow Me" (Matthew 16:24). You may already face so much self-denial and pain that you feel your cross is too heavy to carry. You hoped Jesus would free you from the weight, not call you to drag it along as you seek Him. And that is what the Christian life can feel like—you are hauling this awful burden as you do your best to be a good representative of Jesus.

However, we make a huge mistake as believers when we relegate all that happened at the cross to something in the past. In the spiritual realm, such an attitude can be disastrous—spiritual ignorance is costly indeed. Remember that Jesus said, "Come to Me, all who are weary and burdened, and I will give you rest. Take My yoke upon you and learn from Me, for I am gentle and humble in heart, and you will find rest for your souls" (Matthew 11:28–29). Christ knows how to lead us to the rest, fulfillment, and victory we need. Our lack of understanding of the resurrection has limited its effect on our life.

The truth of the matter is that the benefits of what Jesus accomplished on the cross are not limited to some future date. He helps you *right now.* The resurrection power that raised Jesus from the dead is available to you immediately for everything you are facing. You are *already* in possession of it, so the problem is not in the acquisition but in the application of this awesome power God has provided to you. So how do you take hold of it? After all, you know Jesus gives it to you freely, but perhaps you don't quite feel it working in your life. Your cross feels awful heavy.

Understand that resurrection power is limited by only one thing—*unbelief.* We choose to believe that we will never experience the overcoming power of God in our lives because of our feelings of our own helplessness, unworthiness, and inadequacy. So we live in defeat and are convinced that the Christian life is deficient. But what's truly lacking is our trust in who God is. This is the root of why we sin. And because of it we walk in defeat and serve in weakness. We become discouraged that there is so little fruit from our labors. Our voice reveals our uncertainties; our indecision exposes our fears. Joy is absent from our singing. Conviction is lacking in our witness. We feel so helpless.

This need not be. If you have received the Lord Jesus Christ as your personal Savior, you are the child of the King. The same power that raised the Son of God from the dead and will one day raise your mortal body from the grave is now dwelling within you, ready to be released through you, overcoming every barrier that stands in the way of your obedience to the Lord. But how do you experience this resurrection power? What triggers its release in your life?

Let us go back to the beginning and remember what it was that severed our relationship with God in the first place. If you recall,

Resurrection power is limited by only one thing—unbelief.

the first sin occurred when people chose their way rather than the Lord's. Adam and Eve attempted to accomplish their goals in their own wisdom, despite what the Creator had told them. This is very instructive to us. This world will always pull us away from the life God wants for us.

Therefore, if you want to experience the resurrection power of Christ, the first thing you must do is *yield* your life completely to Jesus. Let me define what I mean when I say "yield." *Yielding* is the deliberate and voluntary transfer of the undivided possession, control, and use of your whole being—spirit, soul, and body—from yourself to Christ. This may sound extreme, but remember that He is both your Creator and your Savior. Not only did He build you and does He know exactly what you need, but He also paid on the cross for your freedom—and it was costly for Him to do so. Therefore, He has your absolute best interest at heart. And His resurrection power can only be entrusted to the person who has first submitted his or her will to God. Otherwise, that power would be employed for selfish ends. And we know that when selfish people wield a great deal of power, it can be disastrous.

This need to yield is why the apostle Paul declared,

I count all things to be loss in view of the surpassing value of knowing Christ Jesus my Lord, for whom I have suffered the loss of all things, and count them mere rubbish, so that I may gain Christ, and may be found in Him, not having a righteousness of my own derived from the Law, but that which is through faith in Christ, the righteousness which comes from God on the basis of faith, that I may know Him and the power of His resurrection and the fellowship of His sufferings, being conformed to His death; if somehow I may attain to the resurrection from the dead. (Philippians 3:8–11)

Paul reconsidered *everything* he thought to be true about what gave his life strength, security, purpose, meaning, and value—not just some of what he believed. The apostle said this exercise was absolutely worth the cost considering what he was gaining, which was experiencing God and His resurrection power–filled life rather than merely knowing about it intellectually. He didn't want anything that would hinder the power of God from flowing through him.

How did he know where those hindrances came from? In Romans 8:11 Paul explained, "The Spirit of God, who raised Jesus from the dead, lives in you. And just as God raised Christ Jesus from the dead, he will give life to your mortal bodies by this same Spirit living within

His resurrection power can only be entrusted to the person who has first submitted his or her will to God.

you" (NLT). The Holy Spirit does so as you spend time with the Lord in the Word and in prayer. Remember, the Word of God always pointed to the cross in a prophetic way. Now that we have seen the cross, we can turn to Scripture to learn all we have received and all Christ has conquered on our behalf. As we read God's Word prayerfully—listening to what the Lord is saying, presenting our questions to Him, and obeying the promptings of His Spirit—the obstacles to Christ's resurrection power are removed.

This kind of evaluation is necessary for all of us as believers. Like the psalmist, we ask God, "Search me, O God, and know my heart; test me and know my anxious thoughts. Point out anything in me that offends you, and lead me along the path of everlasting life" (Psalm 139:23–24 NLT). We don't do that to earn our salvation. When Jesus died on the cross, He paid the debt for our sins *completely*. That means He died for the sins we committed yesterday, today, and forever. Regardless of what mistakes we make in the future, Jesus still accepts us. Our sin after salvation doesn't affect our *eternal standing* before God. Rather, it disrupts our ability to experience Him. You cannot walk with the Lord and continue in ungodly ways—those are two divergent paths. So if you want to be close to your Savior, it's imperative that you choose to walk in *His* direction. It is essential that you *yield* yourself to Him.

With this in mind, the second requirement for experiencing resurrection power is *faith*. We must acknowledge that God is right about whatever is hindering us from knowing Him so we can get on His path—aligned with His purposes and in fellowship with Him. We must trust that He is leading us in the right way, that He will fulfill His promises to us, and that the plan He has for us is truly the very best. And whatever He directs us to do, we obey Him without question, leaving all the consequences to Him.

Hebrews 11:6 explains, "Without faith it is impossible to please Him, for the one who comes to God must believe that He exists, and that He proves to be One who rewards those who seek Him." You can see the two qualifying factors for faith—you must trust that the Lord exists and that He rewards those who seek Him. True faith is not just assurance in a certain outcome; rather, it's absolute confidence in God's unfailing character and ability, regardless of the circumstances. When He speaks, He means what He says and accomplishes what He promises.

This faith in God's character and purposes led Paul to reconsider

When God speaks, He means
what He says and accomplishes
what He promises.

his identity, heritage, accomplishments, strength, wealth, gifts—anything and everything that he was relying on other than Jesus. He discarded it all because he knew the Lord's way was exceedingly, abundantly, far superior. This is the key to every blessing that flows from the Father for you as well.

Resurrection power is released the moment you believe—issued to meet any and every need you might have. You may not see its effects immediately, but you can know for certain that God is working in the unseen to provide for you (Isaiah 64:4; 2 Corinthians 4:18).

With that in mind, I have a statement on the wall in my office to remind me what my responsibility is and what He has provided for me.

This is my commitment: I now absolutely and unconditionally yield all that I am and all that I have to Christ so that He may have His whole will done in my entire life—at every point, no matter what the cost. I accept by faith His acceptance of me and believe His promise that sin shall no longer have dominion over me because of His death on the cross and resurrection from the grave. My surrender is not to be maintained by my efforts but by faith in the power of the Holy Spirit, who dwells within me. By faith, I rest in His ability to provide, direct, protect, and deliver me moment by moment. The work is now His; the rest is now mine. I cease all self-effort to keep myself, to serve Him, or to overcome sin. I obey Him in all things and leave the rest in His care.

I pray you will live by this commitment as well, yielding yourself and having faith in your Savior. Because the same power that raised Christ from the dead is also available to you today for whatever you may be facing. God will work through it to reveal Himself to you and to others in an eternal way—that's what the gift of the cross is all about.

So take hold of it and don't let go. And "to Him who is able to do far more abundantly beyond all that we ask or think, according to the power that works within us, to Him be the glory in the church and in Christ Jesus to all generations forever and ever. Amen" (Ephesians 3:20–21).

The BIG QUESTION

ave you accepted the gift Jesus gave you at the cross?

With arms outstretched, Jesus offers salvation to everyone—but more specifically, to you personally, right now. Friend, have you made the decision to trust Jesus as your Savior? Have you realized that you have sinned against God, that all your good works and promises cannot earn you salvation? Has there ever been a time when you said, "Lord Jesus, I'm asking You to forgive me of my sins. I do believe that Your death on the cross was full payment for my sin debt, and I receive You as my personal Savior and Lord"?

If so, then you've made the greatest choice of your life, because it is an eternal decision. But if you've never taken this step, then come to the cross, humble yourself before the crucified and risen Jesus, and receive the gift of eternal life by faith in His substitutionary death and triumphant resurrection. Draw near to the cross and receive the love that will heal your soul.

How do you do so? Romans 10:9 says, "If you confess with your mouth Jesus as Lord, and believe in your heart that God raised Him from the dead, you will be saved." You can take this step right now. You don't have to know everything about Jesus or what He has done for you. All you must do is accept by faith that what Christ did on the cross was sufficient to save you—to forgive your sins, restore your relationship with the Father, and give you eternal life.

You can tell Him in your own words or use this simple prayer:

Jesus, I believe in You. I believe that You are God, the Lord of heaven, earth, and all that exists. I also believe that You—by taking my sin at the cross and being raised from the dead—have defeated sin and death forever for all who trust in You.

Lord, I ask You to forgive my sins and save me from eternal separation from You. By faith, I accept Your death on the cross and resurrection as sufficient payment for all I have ever done wrong.

Thank You for providing the way for me to know You and to have a relationship with You. Thank You for making me into a new creation, giving me Your Holy Spirit to guide me, and leading me to the new life You have for me. Thank You for giving me an open invitation to enjoy Your presence. Teach me about the cross and the resurrection—about all You did through it and all it means for me and for others. And help me to always follow Your leadership. In Jesus' name, amen.

ABOUT THE AUTHOR

*D*r. Charles Stanley is the pastor emeritus of the First Baptist Church of Atlanta, where he has served for more than 50 years. He is a *New York Times* bestselling author who has written more than 70 books, including the bestselling devotional *Every Day in His Presence*. Dr. Stanley is the founder of In Touch Ministries. The *In Touch with Dr. Charles Stanley* program is transmitted on more than 4,000 television, radio, and satellite networks and stations worldwide, in more than 75 heart languages. The award-winning *In Touch* devotional magazine is printed in four languages and sent to more than one million subscribers monthly. Dr. Stanley's goal is best represented by Acts 20:24: "Life is worth nothing unless I use it for doing the work assigned me by the Lord Jesus—the work of telling others the Good News about God's mighty kindness and love." This is because, as he says, "It is the Word of God and the work of God that changes people's lives."